Many Different Salads

100 RECIPES

Barbara O'neill

Introduction 7

1 Chicken & Pear Salad 8

2 Chicken & Apple Salad 9

3 Chicken Salad 10

4 Red Cabbage Salad 11

5 Broccoli Salad 12

6 Cabbage & Apple Salad 13

7 Tomatoes Salad 14

8 Beans Salad 15

9 Avocado & Corn Salad 16

10 Spinach & Raspberry Salad 17

11 Tasty Salad 18

12 Chickpea Salad 19

13 Rice Salad 20

14 Simple Green Salad 21

15 Pomegranate Salad 22

16 Simple Salad 23

17 Asparagus Salad 24

18 Crab Salad 25

19 Fruit & Feta Cheese Salad 26

20 Easy Salad..*27*
21 Fresh Salad..*28*
22 King Prawns Salad *29*
23 Apple & Lettuce Salad *30*
24 Savoy Cabbage Salad..................................*31*
25 Lemongrass Stalk Salad *32*
26 Light Salad...*33*
27 Avocado & Radish Salad *34*
28 Prawn Meat Salad *35*
29 Fennel & Orange Salad *36*
30 Asian Seafood Salad...................................*37*
31 Potatoes Salad..*38*
32 Easy Summer Salad....................................*40*
33 Green Salad...*41*
34 Green Prawns Salad *42*
35 Avocado & Pecans Salad............................*43*
36 Summer Salad...*44*
37 Zucchini & Rockmelon Salad *45*
38 Tofu Salad...*46*
39 Grilled Chicken Salad *47*
40 Watermelon & Blueberry Salad..................*48*

41 Roasted Vegetable Salad 49

42 Radish & Rocket Salad...................................50

43 Cherry Tomatoes Salad 51

44 Spring Salad..52

45 Tuna & Avocado Salad...................................53

46 Smoked Salmon Salad 54

47 Prawn Salad 55

48 Broccolini & Avocado Salad 56

49 Fantastic Greek Salad 57

50 Mandarins salad 58

51 Winter Salad 59

52 Mixed Salad 60

53 Autumn salad 61

54 Peach Salad...62

55 Apple & Berry Salad......................................63

56 Blue Cheese Salad 64

57 Melon Salad 66

58 Mango Salad 67

59 Shredded Fresh Salad 68

60 Prawn & Cherry Tomatoes Salad 69

61 Bacon Salad 70

62 Radish Salad 71
63 Savoy Cabbage Salad......................................72
64 Mango & Cucumber Salad...............................73
65 Watermelon and Goat's Cheese Salad.......74
66 Cherry & Watermelon Salad.........................75
67 Easy Bean Salad 76
68 Salad with Rocket & Goat's Cheese 77
69 Papaya & Chicken Salad................................78
70 Asparagus & Broccolini Salad......................79
71 Vegetables, Mango & Prawn Salad 80
72 Cherry Tomatoes & Prawn Salad 81
73 Corn Salad 82
74 Cauliflower Salad 83
75 Green Beans & Tomatoes Salad 84
76 Eggplant Salad..85
77 Tomato & Bocconcini Salad 86
78 Bacon & Tomato Salad 87
79 Asparagus & Zucchini Salad 88
80 Spinach Salad 89
81 Tasty Salmon Salad 91
82 Chicken & Avocado Salad............................92

83 Carrot Salad 93

84 Watermelon & Avocado Salad 94

85 Interesting Salad 95

86 Carrot & Cucumber Salad 96

87 Asparagus & Onion Salad............................. 97

88 Rocket & Strawberry Salad 98

89 Pumpkin & Apple Salad 99

90 Apple & Red Cabbage Salad 100

91 Fantastic Green Salad 101

92 Tuna Salad 102

93 Spinach Salad 103

94 Seafood Salad 104

95 Asparagus, Radish & Apple Salad 105

96 Cucumber & Tomato Salad....................... 106

97 Baby Spinach & Carrot Salad 107

98 Prawns & Cucumber Salad 108

99 Radish & Greek Feta Salad....................... 109

100 Tomato & Apple Salad 110

Introduction

This book contains a variety of recipes for Salads representing national cuisine of various countries. Some of them are easy to make and some are not but it is always nice to cook something new, isn't it?

Thanks to this book you will be able to cook your own "home-style" and surprisingly delicious salads. Recipes in this book are excellent for festive parties and for typical home lunches and dinners.

The book provides 100 recipes and I hope these recipes will help you diversify your "cooking" life starting from today! Treat yourself, your friends and beloved ones!

Bon Appetit!

1 Chicken & Pear Salad

Ingredients

- 3 single chicken breast fillets
- 1 tablespoon olive oil
- 1 bunch watercress
- 1 pear cut into thin wedges
- salt, black pepper to taste

Cooking

- Heat the oil in a frying pan over medium-high heat. Season fillets with salt and pepper. Add the chicken to the pan and cook until cooked through. Transfer to a plate.
- Cut the chicken across into the small slices.
- Combine the chicken, watercress and apple in a bowl. Divide among serving plates. Drizzle over olive oil to serve.

2 Chicken & Apple Salad

Ingredients

- 450g chicken breast fillets
- 2 tablespoons whole-egg mayonnaise
- 2 tablespoons yogurt
- 1 teaspoon curry powder
- 3 tablespoons chopped fresh chives
- 2 medium apples, cut into wedges
- 1 cucumber, finely chopped
- salt, to taste

Cooking

- Place chicken in a saucepan. Cover with cold water. Bring to the boil over medium heat. Simmer for 10 minutes or until almost cooked through. Remove from heat. Stand for 5 minutes. Remove chicken from pan. Cool. Slice.
- Combine mayonnaise, yogurt, curry powder and chives in a bowl.
- Arrange apples, cucumber and chicken on a large plate. Drizzle with dressing. Serve.

3 Chicken Salad

Ingredients

- 300g cooked chicken
- 1 Lebanese cucumber, cut into matchsticks
- 4 green onions, cut into matchsticks
- 1 tablespoon soy sauce
- 2 teaspoons sesame oil
- 1 teaspoon curry powder

Cooking

- Shred chicken. Place in a large bowl. Add cucumber, onion and curry powder.
- Combine soy sauce and sesame oil. Pour over salad. Serve.

4 Red Cabbage Salad

Ingredients

- ¼ red cabbage, finely shredded
- ½ tablespoon tamari
- 1 teaspoon lime juice
- ½ teaspoon sesame oil
- 1 tablespoon rice bran oil
- 1 head broccoli thinly sliced
- 2 Lebanese cucumber
- 2 green onions thinly sliced

Cooking

- Place lime juice, sesame oil, rice bran oil and tamari in a small bowl. Whisk.
- Place cabbage, broccoli, Lebanese cucumber, onion and mix in a large bowl. Toss to combine. Add dressing. Serve.

5 Broccoli Salad

Ingredients

- 1 head broccoli thinly sliced
- 2 small pears, cored, thinly sliced
- ½ cup shaved Parmesan cheese
- 1 tablespoon olive oil
- 1 tablespoon honey

Cooking

- Place broccoli, pear and Parmesan in a bowl.
- Place oil and honey in a jar. Shake to combine. Add to rocket mixture. Toss to coat. Serve.

6 Cabbage & Apple Salad

Ingredients

- 1 big apple cut into thin wedges
- 1 tablespoon olive oil
- ½ tablespoon balsamic vinegar
- 2 teaspoons wholegrain mustard
- ¼ red cabbage, finely shredded

Cooking

- Place apple, cabbage and mustard in a bowl.
- Oil and balsamic vinegar shake to combine. Add to rocket mixture. Shake to combine. Serve.

7 Tomatoes Salad

Ingredients

- 350g tomatoes, sliced into rounds
- 1 small red onion, quartered thinly sliced
- 3 tablespoons fresh coriander leaves roughly chopped
- 1 tablespoon extra virgin olive oil
- salt, black pepper to taste

Cooking

- Place tomato, coriander and onion in a bowl. Drizzle with oil. Season with salt and pepper. Toss gently to combine. Serve.

8 Beans Salad

Ingredients

- 300g borlotti beans drained, rinsed
- ¼ red onion thinly sliced
- 1 tablespoon extra-virgin olive oil
- 1 tablespoon red wine vinegar
- 4 tablespoons chopped fresh chives
- salt, black pepper to taste

Cooking

- Combine beans, onion, vinegar, oil, fresh chives and salt and pepper in a bowl. Toss to combine.
- Cover and stand at room temperature for 10 minutes to soften onion. Serve.

9 Avocado & Corn Salad

Ingredients

- 2 large ripe avocados halved peeled finely chopped
- 1 can corn kernels drained
- 2 tablespoons chopped fresh chives
- 2 tablespoons fresh lemon juice
- black pepper to taste

Cooking

- Combine the avocado, corn, fresh chives and lemon juice in a bowl. Serve.

10 Spinach & Raspberry Salad

Ingredients

- ¼ cup olive oil
- 1 tablespoon red wine vinegar
- 150g baby spinach leaves
- 150g fresh raspberries
- 50g chopped walnuts
- 150g feta cheese drained crumbled
- salt, black pepper to taste

Cooking

- Place the oil, vinegar, mustard, salt and pepper in a small screw-top jar. Shake well to combine.
- Place the spinach in a large bowl. Sprinkle with the raspberries, walnuts and feta.
- Drizzle the dressing over the salad. Mix and serve.

11 Tasty Salad

Ingredients

- 1 stick of celery
- 1 small carrot
- 20g fresh basil
- 500g beans
- 1 tablespoon chopped onion
- 120ml extra virgin olive oil
- 50ml white wine vinegar
- salt, black pepper to taste

Cooking

- Trim the celery, peel and trim the carrot, then cut, along with the basil leaves.
- The beans place in a bowl with the celery, carrot, onion and basil. Stir in the olive oil and vinegar.
- Add salt or pepper to taste, if you like.

12 Chickpea Salad

Ingredients

- 400g can chickpeas, drained, rinsed
- 350g broccoli, cut into florets
- 5 radishes sliced
- 30g fresh basil
- 1 tablespoon apple cider vinegar
- 2 tablespoons extra virgin olive oil
- 4 tablespoons chopped fresh chives
- salt, black pepper to taste

Cooking

- Preheat oven to 180C fan forced. Grease a baking tray and line with baking paper. Spread chickpeas over prepared tray. Spray lightly with oil. Bake for 12 minutes or until golden and crisp.
- Place broccoli and edamame in a steamer over a saucepan of simmering water. Cover and steam for 5 minutes. Drain.
- Chop basil and fresh chives.
- Combine the cooked broccoli, radish, basil and fresh chives in a large bowl. Season. Whisk together the oil and vinegar in a bowl. Add the dressing to the salad and gently toss to combine. Top with roasted chickpeas, salt and pepper.

13 Rice Salad

Ingredients

- 300g mixed rice long-grain
- 100g mixed nuts
- 1 bunch fresh basil
- 100g soft prunes
- 2 tablespoons extra virgin olive oil
- salt, black pepper to taste

Cooking

- Cook the rice according to the packet instructions until tender. Drain, then allow to cool.
- Chop the mixed nuts, the basil and the soft prunes.
- Combine with the rice, season with salt and pepper, then drizzle with oil.

14 Simple Green Salad

Ingredients

- 1 soft round lettuce
- 1 little gem lettuce
- 50g basil
- 50g flat-leaf parsley
- 20g mint
- 50g baby spinach leaves
- ½ lemon
- 6 tablespoons extra virgin olive oil
- 3 celery sticks, sliced
- salt, black pepper to taste

Cooking

- To make the dressing, ½ lemon, then squeeze the juice into an empty jar. Add the oil and a pinch of salt and pepper to the jar. Shake well.
- Slice the round lettuce, the gem lettuce, the basil, the flat-leaf parsley, the mint, the baby spinach leaves and the celery sticks.
- Drizzle 2 or 3 tablespoons of the dressing over the leaves and stir gently. Serve.

15 Pomegranate Salad

Ingredients

- 300g medium-grain Bulgur wheat
- 1 pomegranate
- 4 tablespoons extra virgin olive oil
- 2 large handfuls of mixed micro herb and salad leaves
- 1 bunch fresh basil
- 1 small apple

Cooking

- Place the Bulgur wheat in a large bowl, cover with cold water and soak for 2 hours, then drain and put into a bowl.
- Slice the basil and apple, then add to the bowl with the oil.
- Combine with the seeds of pomegranate.
- Mix the micro leaves with the Bulgur wheat, the seeds of pomegranate with the apple and the basil. Serve.

16 Simple Salad

Ingredients

- 150g feta cheese
- 10 ripe cherry tomatoes
- 5 small carrots
- 2 sticks of celery
- 1 little gem lettuce
- 30g basil
- 1 tablespoon balsamic vinegar
- 3 tablespoons extra virgin olive oil

Cooking

- On a board, trim and finely chop the tomatoes, the carrots, the celery, the lettuce and basil.
- Grate the feta cheese and mixing it up.
- Combine the balsamic vinegar and oil in a jam jar.
- Dressing the salad and serve.

17 Asparagus Salad

Ingredients

- ½ bunch of fresh dill
- 1 bunch of asparagus
- 1 bunch of radishes
- 1 small cucumber
- ½ lemon
- extra virgin olive oil

Cooking

- Speed-peel the asparagus and place into the iced water.
- Peel the radishes and cucumber into ribbons, cut into cubes.
- Chop the dill, and place in a bowl. Stir in the lemon juice and a little oil and season well.
- Remove the asparagus from the water and spin until dry, add the radishes and cucumber. Place in the bowl with the dressing and toss. Serve.

18 Crab Salad

Ingredients

- 1 pear
- 2 tangerines
- 1 ripe apple
- 150g white crab meat
- 2 tablespoons extra virgin olive oil
- salt, black pepper to taste

Cooking

- Peel and slice 2 tangerines, pear and apple. Arrange on a plate.
- Add the crab meat.
- Mix all with the oil. Season generously with salt and pepper. Serve.

19 Fruit & Feta Cheese Salad

Ingredients

- 1 ripe peach, halved, pits removed
- 2 firm ripe apricots, halved, pits removed
- 4 tablespoons olive oil
- 1 tablespoon fresh lemon juice
- 150g crumbled feta cheese
- ½ cup chopped, roasted almonds
- 30g basil
- 2 tablespoons butter
- salt, black pepper to taste

Cooking

- Heat the grill. Brush cut sides of peach and apricots with melted butter. Place fruit cut sides down on grill over medium heat. Cook until grill marks form;
- Transfer fruit to the plate; let cool a few minutes. Cut fruit into cubes.
- In a large bowl, beat olive oil and lemon juice, salt and pepper with whisk.
- Cut cheese, roasted almonds and basil.
- Mix all and serve.

20 Easy Salad

Ingredients

- ½ lemons
- 2 tablespoons olive oil
- 1 cucumber, chopped small
- ½ red onion, chopped small
- 200g cherry tomatoes, halved
- 1 can chick peas, drained and rinsed
- salt and black pepper, to taste
- chopped fresh parsley and dill, to taste

Cooking

- Squeeze the juice of lemon into the serving bowl. Add olive oil. Season with salt and pepper.
- Add cucumber, red onion, cherry tomatoes and chick peas to bowl and stir to combine.
- Sprinkle parsley and dill on top. Serve.

21 Fresh Salad

Ingredients

- 1 medium tomato, cut into small slices
- 1 cucumber, chopped
- 50g basil, finely chopped
- 50g dill, finely chopped
- ½ tablespoon balsamic vinegar
- 1 tablespoon olive oil
- salt and black pepper, to taste

Cooking

- Mix the tomatoes and cucumber. Season with salt and pepper. Add olive oil.
- In a small bowl, mix basil and dill; sprinkle over salad. Drizzle with vinegar. Serve.

22 King Prawns Salad

Ingredients

- 200g punnet perino duet tomatoes, halved
- 2 tablespoons extra virgin olive oil
- 100g green beans, trimmed
- 2 tablespoons lemon juice
- 100g bag baby French kale leaves
- 500g cooked king prawns, peeled, tails intact
- salt and black pepper, to taste

Cooking

- Place beans in a bowl. Cover with boiling water. Stand 3 minutes. Drain. Combine lemon juice.
- Toss beans, kale, prawns and tomato together in a large bowl. Season with salt and pepper.
- Divide among serving bowls.
- Drizzle extra virgin olive oil. Serve.

23 Apple & Lettuce Salad

Ingredients

- 1 red apple, cut into bite-size pieces
- 1 small head romaine lettuce, torn into bite-size pieces
- ½ cup walnut halves, toasted
- 2 tablespoons extra virgin olive oil
- 1 teaspoon white wine vinegar
- 1 small finely chopped red onion
- salt, black pepper and ground mustard, to taste

Cooking

- In medium bowl, mix olive oil, vinegar, salt, pepper and mustard with wire whisk; set aside.
- In a large bowl, gently mix salad ingredients. Just before serving, pour dressing over salad. Serve.

24 Savoy Cabbage Salad

Ingredients

- 3 bowls coarsely shredded savoy cabbage
- 200g sliced pastrami, torn
- 150g cheese to taste, shaved
- 1 tablespoon chopped fresh chives
- 3 tablespoons whole egg mayonnaise
- ½ tablespoon fresh lemon juice
- 1 teaspoons horseradish cream
- salt and black pepper, to taste

Cooking

- Place the cabbage, pastrami, cheese and chives in a large bowl. Toss to combine. Drizzle with remaining dressing.
- For the dressing, combine the mayonnaise, lemon juice, horseradish cream, salt and pepper in a small bowl.
- Drizzle with remaining dressing. Serve.

25 Lemongrass Stalk Salad

Ingredients

- 1 lemongrass stalk, white part only, finely chopped
- 1 teaspoon light soy sauce
- 1 baby gem lettuce, leaves separated
- 1 telegraph cucumber, halved, deseeded, sliced
- 150g shredded carrot
- 2 tablespoons extra virgin olive oil
- salt and black pepper, to taste

Cooking

- Combine the lemongrass, soy sauce, lettuce, cucumber and carrot in a bowl.
- Season with salt and pepper.
- Drizzle extra virgin olive oil. Serve.

26 Light Salad

Ingredients

- 200g sour cream
- 3 green shallots, trimmed, thinly sliced
- 1 small telegraph cucumber, halved, deseeded, sliced
- 100g shredded carrot
- 1 red apple, finely chopped
- 50g basil, finely chopped
- salt and black pepper, to taste

Cooking

- Place all the ingredients in a bowl and whisk until combined.
- Season with salt and pepper. Serve.

27 Avocado & Radish Salad

Ingredients

- 1 apple, peeled, sliced
- 1 ½ tablespoon extra virgin olive oil
- 5 radishes, trimmed, cut into wedges
- 1 avocado, stoned, peeled, sliced
- 1 teaspoon lime juice
- 1 tablespoon coarsely chopped chives
- 1 telegraph cucumber, halved, deseeded, sliced
- salt and black pepper, to taste

Cooking

- Place all the ingredients in a bowl and whisk until combined.
- Season with salt and pepper. Serve.

28 Prawn Meat Salad

Ingredients

- 300g cooked prawn meat, chopped
- 1 green shallot, coarsely chopped
- 2 baby cos lettuce, leaves separated
- 30g baby spinach
- 1 teaspoon lime juice
- 2 tablespoons extra virgin olive oil
- salt and black pepper, to taste

Cooking

- Place prawn meat, shallot, lettuce and spinach in a large bowl. Whisk until combined.
- Drizzle the lime juice and olive oil.
- Season with salt and pepper. Serve.

29 Fennel & Orange Salad

Ingredients

- 1 bulb of fennel
- 1 orange
- 1 handful of almonds
- ½ avocado, stoned, peeled
- 1 tablespoon extra virgin olive oil
- salt and black pepper, to taste

Cooking

- Shave the fennel, then place in a bowl of ice water.
- Toast the almonds in a dry frying pan, then crush.
- Peel and thinly slice the oranges and avocado.
- Drain the fennel, spin, then mix with the oranges and avocado.
- Add oil, toasted almonds and season with salt and pepper. Serve.

30 Asian Seafood Salad

Ingredients

- 1 squid, cleaned, from sustainable sources
- 300 g cooked octopus, from sustainable sources
- 10 cooked peeled prawns, from sustainable sources
- 1 ½ tablespoon olive oil
- 1 teaspoon soy sauce
- ½ tablespoon lime juice
- salt and black pepper, to taste

Cooking

- Slice the squid. Heat 1 tablespoon of olive oil in a frying pan over a medium heat, add the squid and cook for 3 to 5 minutes. Add the soy sauce, cook until the squid is tender. Transfer it to a salad bowl.
- Slice the octopus, then place in the salad bowl, with the prawns.
- Add the lime juice and olive oil, salt and pepper. Toss together well. Serve.

31 Potatoes Salad

Ingredients

- 250 g chat potatoes
- 1tablespoon extra virgin olive oil
- 1 green onion, chopped
- 1 tablespoon fresh dill sprigs
- 1 tablespoon fresh flat-leaf parsley leaves
- 3 eggs, sliced
- 1 garlic clove, quartered
- 1 tablespoon lemon juice
- 150 g sour cream
- salt and black pepper, to taste

Cooking

- Place desiree potatoes in a large saucepan. Cover with cold water. Bring to the boil over high heat. Reduce heat to medium. Boil until potatoes are almost tender but not cooked through. Drain. Set aside for 10 minutes to cool. Slice.
- Drizzle potatoes with 1 tablespoon oil. Season with salt and pepper.
- Boil eggs for 12 minutes. Drain. Slice.
- Heat a barbecue grill or chargrill pan on medium-high heat. Cook potatoes, in batches, for 3 minutes each side or until

golden and cooked through. Transfer to a heatproof serving plate.
- Meanwhile, chopped onion, dill, parsley, eggs and garlic. Add remaining oil and lemon juice. Season with salt and pepper.
- Pour over the potatoes with sour cream. Drizzle with dressing. Serve.

32 Easy Summer Salad

Ingredients

- 2 ripe mangoes
- 1 tablespoon fresh lime juice
- ½ red onion, finely chopped
- 3 tablespoons fresh coriander leaves
- 1 tablespoon extra virgin olive oil
- salt and black pepper, to taste

Cooking

- Peel mangoes and chop the flesh into 0,5 cm pieces.
- Combine the mango, onion, coriander, olive oil and lime juice in a small bowl. Season with salt and pepper. Serve.

33 Green Salad

Ingredients

- 1 bunch rocket
- 1 frisee curly endive
- 1 tablespoon snipped chives
- 2 tablespoons fresh dill, chopped
- 1 tablespoon flat-leaf parsley, chopped
- 2 tablespoons lemon juice
- 3 tablespoons baby spinach
- 3 tablespoons olive oil
- salt and black pepper, to taste

Cooking

- Chop all herbs, as you like and mix.
- In a big bowl, whisk the lemon juice and oil with some salt and pepper. Pour over the salad and combine. Serve at once.

34 Green Prawns Salad

Ingredients

- 150g baby rocket
- 200g vine-ripened cherry tomatoes
- 2 teaspoons sweet paprika
- 1 garlic clove, crushed
- 3 tablespoons olive oil
- 25 green prawns, peeled, tails left intact
- 1 tablespoon lemon juice
- salt and black pepper, to taste
- 3 or 4 tablespoons mayonnaise
- 1 tablespoon fresh lemon juice

Cooking

- Heat a large frying pan over medium-high heat. Spray the prawns with oil. Season and cook the prawns turning once, for 3 minutes or until the prawns aren't cooked through. Transfer to a plate.
- Combine the paprika, garlic, lemon juice and oil in a large bowl. Add the cherry tomatoes and toss until well coated. Add the mayonnaise and prawns. Season. Set aside for 15 minutes.
- Arrange the rocket on a serving platter. Top with a mixture of the prawns and tomatoes. Serve.

35 Avocado & Pecans Salad

Ingredients

- 1 large avocado, sliced
- 60g pecans, roughly chopped
- 1 tablespoon honey
- 2 tablespoons extra virgin olive oil
- 150g baby rocket
- salt and black pepper, to taste

Cooking

- Preheat oven to 175C fan-forced. Line a baking tray with baking paper.
- Place pecans on prepared tray. Drizzle with honey. Bake for 10 minutes or until golden. Set aside to cool.
- Place oil in a small bowl. Season with salt and pepper. Stir. Place rocket on a serving plate. Arrange avocado on top. Drizzle with dressing and sprinkle with pecans. Serve.

36 Summer Salad

Ingredients

- 2 tablespoons extra virgin olive oil
- ½ small bunch silverbeet, stems discarded
- 250g broccoli, trimmed, thinly sliced
- 1 red apple, cut into matchsticks
- 1 green onion, trimmed, thinly sliced
- 5 fresh mint leaves
- 50g sunflower seeds, toasted
- 1 tablespoon lemon juice
- salt and black pepper, to taste

Cooking

- Place oil and lemon juice in a small bowl. Season with salt and pepper. Stir.
- Shred silverbeet leaves. Place silverbeet, broccoli, apple, onion and mint in a serving bowl. Toss to combine. Drizzle with dressing and sprinkle with sunflowers over seeds. Serve.

37 Zucchini & Rockmelon Salad

Ingredients

- 1 zucchini, cut into long matchsticks
- 350g rockmelon, seeded, peeled, cut into thin wedges
- 1 spring onion, thinly sliced
- ¼ cup mint leaves
- ¼ cup flat-leaf parsley leaves
- 2 tablespoons extra virgin olive oil
- 1 tablespoon lemon juice
- 1 tablespoon mustard
- salt and black pepper, to taste

Cooking

- Place zucchini, rockmelon, spring onion, mint and parsley in a bowl. Toss to combine.
- Mix lemon juice, mustard and oil in a small bowl. Season.
- Divide salad among serving plates. Drizzle with the dressing. Serve.

38 Tofu Salad

Ingredients

- 2 zucchini, thinly sliced lengthways
- 250g firm tofu, thinly sliced
- 3 tablespoons extra virgin olive oil
- 2 tablespoons balsamic vinegar
- 1 garlic clove, crushed
- 150g cherry tomatoes, sliced
- 1 spring onion, thinly sliced
- salt and black pepper, to taste

Cooking

- Preheat a chargrill on high. Spray zucchini and tofu with olive oil. Cook for 1 or 2 minutes each side or until charred.
- Combine the oil, vinegar and garlic in a jar and shake until well combined. Season.
- Divide zucchini and tofu among serving plates. Top with tomato. Sprinkle with spring onion and drizzle with the dressing.

39 *Grilled Chicken Salad*

Ingredients

- 2 chicken breasts fillets
- 2 baby cos lettuce, washed, leaves separated
- 50g Parmesan cheese
- 1 garlic clove, quartered
- 4 tablespoons olive oil
- 3 tablespoons lemon juice
- salt, black pepper, to taste

Cooking

- Heat a chargrill on high. Cut slits in the top of the chicken. Cook on grill for 7 minutes each side or until cooked through. Transfer to a plate. Cover with foil and set aside for 5 minutes to rest.
- Mix garlic, oil and lemon juice. Season.
- Thinly slice the chicken. Divide the lettuce, among serving bowls. Put fillet. Drizzle with dressing. Sprinkle with the Parmesan and season to serve.

40 Watermelon & Blueberry Salad

Ingredients

- 4 tablespoons caster sugar
- 90 ml water
- 1 tablespoon lemon juice
- 1 kg watermelon, peeled, quartered
- 125 g blueberries
- 6 mint leaves
- 1 large avocado, sliced

Cooking

- Combine the sugar and 90 ml water in a small saucepan. Cook over medium heat, stirring, until sugar dissolves. Bring to the boil. Cook for 2 minutes. Set aside to cool.
- Combine the syrup and lemon juice in a bowl.
- Cut the watermelon and avocado into small wedges about 1,5 cm thick. Arrange watermelon on a large serving platter with blueberries, avocado and mint. Drizzle with syrup. Serve.

41 Roasted Vegetable Salad

Ingredients

- 300g baby carrots, peeled, halved lengthways
- 2 baby beetroot, peeled, quartered
- 2 tablespoon olive oil
- 1 small red onion, cut into thin wedges
- 50g fresh ricotta
- 1 tablespoon lemon juice
- ¼ cup mayonnaise
- 1 garlic clove, crushed
- salt and black pepper, to taste

Cooking

- Preheat oven to 180C. Combine the carrots, beetroot and half the oil in a medium baking dish. Roast for 35 minutes or until tender.
- Place roasted vegetable mixture among serving plates. Top with onion.
- Combine lemon juice, mayonnaise, oil and garlic in a bowl. Drizzle over salad. Season with salt and pepper. Serve.

42 Radish & Rocket Salad

Ingredients

- 100g feta, crumbled
- 2 or 3 tablespoons olive oil
- 2 tablespoons coarsely chopped dill
- 100g Coles Australian Baby Rocket
- 6 radishes, trimmed, thinly sliced
- 1 small red onion, thinly sliced
- salt and black pepper, to taste

Cooking

- Put the oil and dill in a screw-top jar and shake until well combined. Season.
- Place the rocket, radish and onion in the bowl. Drizzle with the dressing and toss to combine. Divide the salad among serving plates and sprinkle with feta. Serve.

43 Cherry Tomatoes Salad

Ingredients

- 50g Coles Australian Leaf Salad
- 5 radishes, thinly sliced
- 150g cherry tomatoes, halved
- 40g shaved Parmesan
- 2 tablespoons extra virgin olive oil
- 1 tablespoon lemon juice
- salt and black pepper, to taste

Cooking

- Arrange salad leaves, radish and tomatoes on a serving platter. Sprinkle with Parmesan.
- Combine oil and lemon juice in a bowl. Drizzle over the salad on the platter and season. Serve.

44 Spring Salad

Ingredients

- 1 avocado, sliced
- 2 hard-boiled eggs, halved
- 30g shaved Parmesan
- 1 tablespoon olive oil
- chopped fresh chives, to serve
- salt and black pepper, to taste

Cooking

- Arrange avocado and hard-boiled eggs in the plates. Sprinkle with shaved Parmesan, drizzle with oil and season with salt and pepper. Sprinkle with chopped fresh chives. Serve.

45 Tuna & Avocado Salad

Ingredients

- 1 garlic clove, crushed
- 1 tablespoon olive oil
- 225g can tuna in oil, drained, flaked
- 1 small red onion, finely chopped
- 4 small radishes, thinly sliced
- 1 avocado, quartered
- 60g goat's cheese
- salt and black pepper, to taste

Cooking

- Spread the tuna, onion, radish and avocado over the serving plates.
- Combine the garlic and oil in a small bowl. Season.
- Top the goat's cheese over the salad. Drizzle with the dressing and serve.

46 Smoked Salmon Salad

Ingredients

- ½ cup natural yogurt
- 2 tablespoons chopped fresh continental parsley
- 2 tablespoons chopped fresh chives
- 1 tablespoon fresh lemon juice
- 100g baby spinach
- 1 avocado, sliced
- 180g sliced salt-reduced smoked salmon
- salt and black pepper, to taste

Cooking

- Process the yogurt, parsley, chives and in a food processor until smooth. Season with pepper.
- Place lemon juice and a pinch of salt in a bowl.
- Combine the spinach and avocado in a large bowl. Divide among plates. Top with salmon. Drizzle with the "green" dressing and "salt" lemon juice. Serve.

47 Prawn Salad

Ingredients

- 500g raw banana prawns, peeled leaving tails intact
- ¼ red cabbage, shredded
- ½ cup mint leaves
- 2 tablespoons fish sauce
- 2 garlic cloves, crushed
- ½ tablespoon olive oil
- salt and black pepper, to taste

Cooking

- Combine prawns, fish sauce and garlic, in a medium bowl. Place in the fridge for 10 minutes to chill.
- Meanwhile, to make the dressing, place olive oil, cabbage and mint leaves in a screw-top jar. Seal and shake to combine.
- Heat a greased barbecue grill or chargrill on high. Cook prawns for 3 minutes each side or until prawns curl and are cooked through.
- Add prawns in the bowl with the dressing and toss to combine. Season. Transfer to a serving dish. Serve.

48 Broccolini & Avocado Salad

Ingredients

- 2 bunches broccolini, trimmed
- 60g baby spinach
- 1 avocado, thinly sliced
- 2 tablespoons vegetable oil
- 1 teaspoon sesame seeds, toasted
- ½ cup fresh coriander leaves
- 2 tablespoons natural almond kernels, roughly chopped
- salt and black pepper, to taste

Cooking

- Cook broccolini in a saucepan of boiling, salted water for 2 minutes or until just tender. Drain. Refresh under cold water. Drain.
- Place spinach on serving plates. Top with broccolini and avocado. Season with salt and pepper. Whisk oil and sesame seeds together in a small jug. Spoon dressing over broccolini mixture. Sprinkle coriander and almonds. Serve.

49 Fantastic Greek Salad

Ingredients

- 2 tablespoons extra virgin olive oil
- 2 Lebanese cucumbers, halved lengthways, thinly sliced
- 300g mixed baby tomatoes, halved
- ½ cup drained roasted capsicum strips
- ½ cup kalamata olives
- 1 tablespoon lemon juice
- 1 baby cos lettuce, leaves separated
- 100g feta, crumbled
- 1 tablespoon fresh oregano leaves
- salt and black pepper, to taste

Cooking

- Combine cucumber, tomato, capsicum, olives, juice and oil in a bowl. Toss gently to combine.
- Divide lettuce among serving bowls. Top with vegetables mixture, then feta and oregano. Season.

50 Mandarins salad

Ingredients

- 1 tablespoon extra virgin olive oil
- 1 baby fennel, thinly sliced lengthways
- 1 avocado, thinly sliced
- 2 mandarins, peeled, sliced crossways
- 120g bag 4-leaf salad mix
- 1 tablespoon pepitas
- salt and black pepper, to taste

Cooking

- Combine avocado, mandarin, salad mix and fennel on a serving platter. Drizzle with oil and season. Sprinkle with pepitas. Serve.

51 Winter Salad

Ingredients

- 2 eggs
- 1 large carrot, peeled, cut into long thin strips
- 1 large beetroot, peeled, cut into thin strips
- ¼ small head broccoli, thinly sliced lengthways
- 2 tablespoons fresh orange juice
- 2 tablespoons extra virgin olive oil
- 1 tablespoon fresh lemon juice
- 1 garlic clove, smashed
- salt and black pepper, to taste

Cooking

- For the dressing, combine all the ingredients in a small screw top jar. Season and combine. Set aside.
- Place the eggs in a saucepan and cover with boiling water. Bring to the boil, stirring occasionally. Cook for 10 minutes. Drain and run eggs under cold water. Peel. Slice eggs in half.
- Combine the carrot, beetroot and broccoli in a large bowl. Drizzle with the dressing and toss to coat. Divide among serving plates. Top with egg. Serve.

52 Mixed Salad

Ingredients

- 200g mixed medley tomatoes, sliced
- 120g pkt Coles Australian 4 Leaf Salad
- 150g tub bocconcini, drained, thinly sliced
- 2 tablespoons balsamic dressing
- salt and black pepper, to taste

Cooking

- Arrange the tomatoes, salad leaves and bocconcini on a serving platter. Drizzle with dressing. Season. Serve.

53 Autumn salad

Ingredients

- 2 bunches Dutch carrots, thinly sliced
- 1 tablespoon olive oil
- ½ cup walnut halves
- 1 tablespoon orange juice
- 1 small orange
- 1 tablespoon white wine vinegar
- 1 small fennel, finely shaved
- 120g pkt Coles Australian Baby Rocket
- 100g goat's cheese, crumbled
- salt and black pepper, to taste

Cooking

- Arrange the carrots, walnuts and fennel on the dish and drizzle with the oil. Season.
- Place the orange juice, vinegar and remaining oil in a screw-top jar and shake until well combined. Season.
- Combine the carrots, fennel, orange segments and rocket in a serving bowl. Drizzle with a little of the dressing. Toss to combine. Sprinkle with the goat's cheese. Serve.

54 Peach Salad

Ingredients

- 2 small yellow peaches, halved, stones removed
- 50g baby rocket
- ½ x 210g tub traditional bocconcini, torn
- 1 teaspoon honey
- ½ cup walnut halves
- 1 tablespoon lemon juice
- 1 tablespoon finely chopped fresh basil leaves
- 2 tablespoons extra virgin olive oil
- salt and black pepper, to taste

Cooking

- Heat a chargrill pan over medium-high heat. Place peach, cut-side down, in pan. Chargrill for 2 minutes or until charred. Transfer to a large plate.
- Make dressing, whisk honey, lemon juice and oil together in a small bowl until honey dissolves. Add basil. Season with salt and pepper.
- Arrange the baby rocket, peach and bocconcini on a large serving plate. Drizzle over dressing and sprinkle with walnut. Serve.

55 Apple & Berry Salad

Ingredients

- 1 tablespoon extra virgin olive oil
- 1 tablespoon lemon juice
- 2 small red apples, halved, cored, sliced
- 100 g mixed salad leaves
- 125g blueberries
- 125g raspberries
- 100 g goat's cheese, crumbled
- salt and black pepper, to taste

Cooking

- Whisk oil and lemon juice in a large bowl. Toss apple in the dressing.
- Place salad leaves on a serving plate. Arrange apple, blueberries and raspberries over salad leaves. Top with cheese. Season and serve.

56 Blue Cheese Salad

Ingredients

- 2 eggs
- 1 bunch asparagus, trimmed, cut into thirds
- 1 avocado, chopped
- 100g blueberries
- 2 tablespoons chopped fresh chives
- 1 ½ tablespoons light whole-egg mayonnaise
- 1 tablespoon light sour cream
- 1 tablespoon lemon juice
- 50g roquefort blue cheese, crumbled
- salt and black pepper, to taste

Cooking

- Place the eggs in a saucepan and cover with boiling water. Bring to the boil, stirring occasionally. Cook for 10 minutes. Drain and run eggs under cold water. Peel. Slice eggs in half.
- Meanwhile, place asparagus in a medium heatproof bowl. Cover with boiling water. Stand for 3 minutes or until bright green and tender. Drain and refresh.
- Place mayonnaise, lemon juice, sour cream and cheese in a small food processor. Season with salt and pepper. Process until smooth.

- Arrange avocado, blueberries, asparagus and eggs on a serving platter. Drizzle with dressing. Sprinkle with chives. Serve.

57 Melon Salad

Ingredients

- 300g rockmelon
- 1 Lebanese cucumber, thinly sliced
- 2 tablespoons fresh oregano leaves
- 5 fresh basil leaves
- 1 tablespoon extra virgin olive oil
- 2 tablespoons white wine vinegar
- 100g feta, cut into cubes
- salt and black pepper, to taste

Cooking

- Arrange cucumber, oregano and basil on a serving plate.
- Cut melon, peel and discard skin and seeds. Cut into slices. Place on the plate with cucumber, oregano and basil.
- Whisk oil and vinegar together in a small jug. Season with salt and pepper. Top salad with feta and drizzle with dressing. Serve.

58 Mango Salad

Ingredients

- 1 Lebanese cucumber, thinly sliced
- ½ garlic clove, crushed
- 1 mango, thinly sliced
- 1 small red onion, thinly sliced
- salt and black pepper, to taste

Cooking

- Arrange the cucumber, mango, onion and garlic on a serving platter. Drizzle with the oil. Season and serve.

59 Shredded Fresh Salad

Ingredients

- 2 small carrots, peeled, cut into noodles using a spiraliser
- 1 Lebanese cucumber, halved lengthways, seeds removed, thinly sliced
- 100g red cabbage, finely shredded
- ½ bunch fresh coriander, leaves picked
- ½ tablespoons fresh lime juice
- 1 tablespoons olive oil
- salt and black pepper, to taste

Cooking

- For the dressing, combine the oil and lime juice in a small bowl.
- Combine the carrot, cucumber and coriander in a large bowl. Drizzle with dressing. Toss to combine. Season and serve.

60 Prawn & Cherry Tomatoes Salad

Ingredients

- 400g green prawns, peeled, cooked, tails intact
- 250g cherry tomatoes, halved
- 1 small red onion, thinly sliced into rounds
- 1 ½ tablespoons extra virgin olive oil
- 1 small radicchio
- 2 tablespoons fresh continental parsley leaves
- salt and black pepper, to taste

Cooking

- Place the prawns to a large bowl. Add the tomato and onion. Drizzle with oil. Season.
- Separate the radicchio leaves and arrange on a large serving platter. Top with the prawns mixture and sprinkle with parsley. Serve.

61 Bacon Salad

Ingredients

- 10 rashers streaky bacon
- 150g finely shredded red cabbage
- 150g finely shredded savoy cabbage
- 2 tablespoons extra virgin olive oil
- 3 soft-boiled eggs, peeled, halved
- salt and black pepper, to taste

Cooking

- Heat oil in a pan over high heat. Cook bacon for 1 minute each side or until browned and crisp. Transfer to a plate lined with paper towel.
- Place the eggs in a saucepan and cover with boiling water. Bring to the boil, stirring occasionally. Cook for 10 minutes. Drain and run eggs under cold water. Peel. Slice eggs as you like.
- Divide cabbage mixture among serving bowls. Add bacon and eggs. Drizzle with oil and season. Serve.

62 Radish Salad

Ingredients

- 1 baby cos lettuce, leaves separated
- 1 tablespoon mayonnaise
- 1 tablespoon creme fraiche
- 1 teaspoon lemon juice
- 5 radishes, trimmed, thinly sliced
- 1 spring onion, sliced
- salt and black pepper, to taste

Cooking

- Combine mayonnaise, creme fraiche and juice in a bowl. Season with salt and pepper.
- Place lettuce on a large serving platter. Top with radish and onion. Drizzle with dressing. Serve.

63 Savoy Cabbage Salad

Ingredients

- ½ small savoy cabbage, finely shredded
- 1 large apple, finely chopped
- 1 Lebanese cucumber, halved lengthways, deseeded, thinly sliced
- 1 ½ tablespoons olive oil
- 1 ½ tablespoons lemon juice
- 1 garlic clove, crushed
- salt and black pepper, to taste

Cooking

- Combine cabbage, apple and cucumber in a large bowl.
- Whisk oil, lemon juice, garlic and salt and pepper together in a bowl until well combined.
- Drizzle the salad with dressing. Serve.

64 Mango & Cucumber Salad

Ingredients

- 2 Lebanese cucumbers
- 3 tablespoons fresh coriander leaves
- 2 tablespoons fresh mint leaves
- 2 mangoes, thinly sliced
- ½ tablespoon lime juice
- 1 teaspoon olive oil
- 1 tablespoon roughly chopped roasted cashews

Cooking

- Thinly slice cucumbers.
- Mix cucumbers, coriander, mint and mango. Toss to combine.
- Whisk lime juice and oil in a jug. Season with salt and pepper. Drizzle over salad. Toss to combine. Sprinkle with cashews. Serve.

65 Watermelon and Goat's Cheese Salad

Ingredients

- 300g watermelon, peeled, cut into small cubes
- 100g Coles Australian Goat's Cheese, crumbled
- 1 small red apple, thinly sliced
- 120g pkt Coles Australian 4 Leaf Salad
- 1 tablespoon olive oil
- ¼ cup orange juice
- salt and black pepper, to taste

Cooking

- Place the salad leaves, watermelon and goat's cheese in a large serving bowl.
- Combine the oil and orange juice in a bowl. Drizzle over the salad. Season and serve.

66 Cherry & Watermelon Salad

Ingredients

- 200g fresh cherries, halved, stones removed
- ½ small seedless watermelon, to cut into 1cm-thick slices
- 120g raspberries
- 120g blueberries
- 2 tablespoons caster sugar
- 1 tablespoon lime juice
- ½ teaspoon vanilla bean paste, or to taste
- 50ml water

Cooking

- To make the syrup, combine the sugar, lime juice and vanilla in a saucepan. Add water. Place over low heat and cook, stirring occasionally, for 3 minutes or until syrup thickens slightly. Remove from heat. Add the cherries, stir and cool.
- Arrange the watermelon, raspberries and blueberries on a serving platter. Spoon over the cherries and syrup. Serve.

67 Easy Bean Salad

Ingredients

- 1 small garlic clove, crushed
- 200g mixed medley tomatoes, thinly sliced
- 200g bocconcini, torn
- 200g can cannellini beans, rinsed, drained
- ½ tablespoon white wine vinegar
- ½ tablespoon olive oil
- salt and black pepper, to taste

Cooking

- Arrange tomatoes, bocconcini and beans on a serving platter.
- Combine the oil, garlic and vinegar. Season.
- Drizzle over the salad. Serve.

68 Salad with Rocket & Goat's Cheese

Ingredients

- 100g Coles Australian Goat's Cheese, crumbled
- 1 tablespoon extra-virgin olive oil
- ½ tablespoon fresh lemon juice
- 1 tablespoon shallot, finely chopped
- 100g baby rocket leaves
- 5 fresh basil leaves, torn
- 1 tablespoon fresh oregano leaves
- salt and black pepper, to taste

Cooking

- Place the oil and lemon juice, shallot, basil and oregano in a bowl. Season. Set aside for 10 minutes.
- Arrange the baby rocket leaves on a serving platter. Drizzle the salad with dressing. Season with salt and pepper.
- Scatter the Goat's Cheese over the salad and serve.

69 Papaya & Chicken Salad

Ingredients

- 400g chicken thigh fillets, trimmed
- 1 garlic clove, crushed
- 2 tablespoons olive oil
- 1 small apple, peeled, cut into wedges
- 1 small papaya, peeled, cut into wedges
- 1 tablespoon lime juice
- salt and black pepper, to taste

Cooking

- Preheat a barbecue grill or char-grill pan on high. Lightly spray with oil and season. Cook the chicken for 3-4 minutes each side or until cooked through. Transfer to a plate and set aside.
- Slice chicken and spread over serving plates. Top with apple, crushed garlic (to taste) and papaya.
- Drizzle with lime juice and oil. Serve.

70 Asparagus & Broccolini Salad

Ingredients

- 1 bunch asparagus, trimmed, halved
- 1 bunch broccolini, trimmed, halved lengthways
- 1 tablespoon rice wine vinegar
- 2 tablespoons salt-reduced soy sauce
- 1 tablespoon olive oil
- 50g baby spinach
- 2 tablespoons roughly chopped fresh chives
- black pepper, to taste

Cooking

- Cook asparagus and broccolini in the boiling water for 2-3 minutes of cooking time. Drain. Rinse under cold water. Drain. Transfer to a bowl.
- Place oil, pepper, vinegar and soy sauce in a small bowl. Stir to combine.
- Add dressing, baby spinach and chives to asparagus and broccolini. Toss to combine. Serve.

71 Vegetables, Mango & Prawn Salad

Ingredients

- 1 carrot, peeled, cut into long matchsticks
- 1 mango, peeled, thinly sliced
- 0,5 kg cooked prawns, peeled leaving tails intact
- 1 Lebanese cucumber, thinly sliced diagonally
- 1 red onion, thinly sliced
- 1 cup coriander leaves
- 1 tablespoon lemon juice
- 1 tablespoon fish sauce
- 1 tablespoon olive oil
- salt and black pepper, to taste

Cooking

- Arrange mango, prawns, cucumber, carrot, onion and coriander on a serving platter.
- To make the dressing, combine the lemon juice, fish sauce and olive oil in a screw-top jar. Shake until well combined. Drizzle over salad. Serve.

72 Cherry Tomatoes & Prawn Salad

Ingredients

- 250g fresh cherry tomatoes, halved
- 50ml extra virgin olive oil
- 1 teaspoon red wine vinegar
- 1 Lebanese cucumber, thinly sliced diagonally
- 200g cooked black tiger prawns, peeled, tails intact
- salt and black pepper, to taste

Cooking

- Arrange tomatoes, prawns and cucumber on a serving platter.
- To make the dressing, combine the oil and vinegar in a screw-top jar. Shake until well combined. Drizzle over salad. Serve.

73 Corn Salad

Ingredients

- 1 cup sweet corn (in a can)
- ½ tablespoon olive oil
- 2 tablespoons mayonnaise
- 1 tablespoon sour cream
- 1 Lebanese cucumber, thinly sliced diagonally
- ½ cup coriander leaves, finely chopped
- 1 small napa cabbage (wombok), cut into long matchsticks
- 2 spring onions, thinly sliced
- salt and black pepper, to taste

Cooking

- In a small bowl, whisk mayonnaise, sour cream, and oil. Season with salt and pepper.
- Spoon the corn over a serving platter. Spoon the crema over the top. Sprinkle with the coriander, spring onion, cabbage and cucumber. Serve.

74 Cauliflower Salad

Ingredients

- 1 cauliflower, cut into florets
- 200g Perino grape tomatoes, halved lengthways
- 2 tablespoons olive oil
- 100g spinach leaves
- ½ tablespoon lemon juice
- sweet red pepper, to taste
- salt and black pepper, to taste

Cooking

- Preheat oven to 220C. Line a baking tray with baking paper. Spray with oil.
- Place cauliflower and tomato on prepared tray. Season. Bake for 10 minutes or until cauliflower is lightly browned.
- Place cauliflower, spinach and tomato in a bowl. Combine juice, vinegar, oil and sweet pepper in a small bowl. Season. Add dressing to salad and serve.

75 Green Beans & Tomatoes Salad

Ingredients

- 1 cup Greek-style yogurt
- 350g green beans, cooked
- 1 tablespoon olive oil
- 350g mixed medley tomatoes, halved
- ½ cup fresh coriander leaves
- 3 tablespoons fresh flat-leaf parsley leaves
- 2 tablespoons crushed crackers, or to taste
- salt and black pepper, to taste

Cooking

- In a large bowl, whisk oil and yogurt. Season with salt and pepper. Add green beans, tomatoes, coriander, parsley and toss to coat.
- Spread yogurt sauce over base of a serving platter. Place bean and tomatoes on top of sauce. Sprinkle with crushed crackers and serve.

76 Eggplant Salad

Ingredients

- 1 Lebanese cucumber, thinly sliced diagonally
- 3 Lebanese eggplants, halved lengthways
- 3 tablespoons extra virgin olive oil
- ½ lemon, juiced
- 1 bunch radishes, halved, stems intact
- 200g feta, crumbled
- salt and black pepper, to taste

Cooking

- Heat a chargrill pan or barbecue grill over high heat. Brush the eggplant with 1 tablespoon oil. Cook, turning often, for 10 minutes or until softened. Set aside to cool.
- Combine the lemon juice and 2 tablespoons oil in a small bowl. Season.
- Divide the eggplant, cucumber, radish and feta among serving plates. Drizzle with the dressing. Serve.

77 Tomato & Bocconcini Salad

Ingredients

- 350g mixed grape tomatoes, chopped
- ½ cup extra virgin olive oil
- 100g spinach leaves
- 1 apple, peeled, thinly sliced
- 100g buffalo mozzarella, drained, torn
- 200g bocconcini, drained
- salt and black pepper, to taste

Cooking

- Divide the tomatoes, spinach, apple and bocconcini among serving plates.
- Sprinkle with mozzarella. Drizzle with oil and season. Serve.

78 Bacon & Tomato Salad

Ingredients

- 250g rindless middle bacon rashers, cut into lardons
- 150g mayonnaise
- 1 tablespoons lemon juice
- 200g tomatoes medley mix, quartered
- 1 Lebanese cucumber, thinly sliced diagonally
- salt and black pepper, to taste

Cooking

- Cook the bacon, stirring often, in a non-stick frying pan over medium heat for 10 minutes or until golden and crisp. Transfer to a plate.
- Place the bacon in a large bowl. Add the mayonnaise and lemon juice. Season and toss until combined. Add the tomatoes and cucumber. Serve.

79 Asparagus & Zucchini Salad

Ingredients

- 1 bunch asparagus, trimmed
- 1 medium zucchini, peeled
- 1 tablespoon extra virgin olive oil
- 1 tablespoon lemon juice
- salt and black pepper, to taste
- 2 tablespoons skinless hazelnuts, chopped
- ½ teaspoon sweet paprika

Cooking

- Heat a barbecue grill or chargrill pan on high heat. Toss asparagus and zucchini in oil. Season with salt and pepper. Cook for 4 to 5 minutes, each side, or until lightly charred and just tender. Transfer to a plate.
- Arrange asparagus and zucchini on a serving plate. Drizzle with lemon juice and oil. Sprinkle paprika and hazelnut on top. Serve.

80 Spinach Salad

Ingredients

- 250g pkt frozen spinach, thawed
- 50g finely grated Parmesan
- 1 tablespoon extra virgin olive oil
- 250g cooked or drained canned beetroot, peeled, quartered
- 120g baby rocket leaves
- 100g goat's cheese, crumbled
- 1 tablespoon lemon juice
- salt and black pepper, to taste

Cooking

- Squeeze the spinach as possible. Place the spinach in a large bowl. Add the Parmesan and stir to combine. Season. Roll the spinach mixture into a ball. Place on a plate.
- Heat a frying pan over medium heat. Add 1 teaspoon of the oil to the pan and cook spinach for 3 minutes each side. Transfer to a plate.
- Place the beetroot and rocket in a bowl. Combine the remaining oil and lemon juice in a small bowl. Season. Drizzle over the beetroot mixture in the bowl and toss to combine. Divide among serving plates.

Top with goat's cheese and spinach mixture. Serve.

81 Tasty Salmon Salad

Ingredients

- 150g snow peas, trimmed, halved diagonally
- 1 avocado, peeled, thinly sliced
- 185g pkt Coles Tasmanian Hot Smoked Salmon Fillets
- 1 tablespoon lime juice
- 1 tablespoon olive oil
- salt and black pepper, to taste

Cooking

- Cook the snow peas in a saucepan of boiling water for 2 min or until bright green and just tender. Refresh under cold water. Drain.
- Combine the snow peas, avocado and salmon in a large bowl. Divide among serving bowls.
- Place lime juice and oil in a screw-top jar. Shake well to combine. Drizzle the dressing over the salad. Season and serve.

82 Chicken & Avocado Salad

Ingredients

- 200g smoked chicken breast
- 1 Lebanese cucumbers, halved lengthways, diagonally sliced
- 1 avocado, thinly sliced
- 1 garlic clove, peeled, chopped
- 3 sprigs fresh tarragon, leaves finely chopped
- 1 tablespoon olive oil
- salt and black pepper, to taste

Cooking

- Preheat the oven to 150C fan forced. Place the breast on the prepared tray. Heat in the oven for 15 minutes or until warmed through. Thinly slice it.
- Place the garlic, tarragon, oil, salt and pepper in a screw-top jar. Shake well to combine.
- Arrange the lettuce, chicken, cucumber and avocado on a large serving platter. Drizzle with the garlic mixture. Serve.

83 Carrot Salad

Ingredients

- 3 carrots, peeled, cut into noodles using a spiraliser
- 2 zucchini, cut into noodles using a spiraliser
- 100g goat's cheese, crumbled
- 100g walnuts, toasted
- 2 tablespoons fresh lemon juice
- 1 tablespoon fresh orange juice
- 3 tablespoons extra virgin olive oil
- 2 garlic cloves, finely chopped
- salt and black pepper, to taste

Cooking

- For the dressing, whisk the lemon juice, olive oil, garlic and orange juice together in a small bowl. Season.
- Arrange the carrot, zucchini and goat's cheese on a large platter. Sprinkle with the walnuts. Drizzle with the dressing and serve.

84 Watermelon & Avocado Salad

Ingredients

- 1 avocado, peeled, thinly sliced
- 1 cup mint leaves
- 200g Greek-style yogurt
- ¼ watermelon, thinly sliced, cut into wedges
- 1 Lebanese cucumber, cut into ribbons
- 2 tablespoons coriander leaves
- 3 tablespoons pistachios, chopped
- sugar or honey, to taste

Cooking

- Chop the mint. Add the yogurt and process until smooth. Transfer to a bowl and season.
- Arrange the watermelon, cucumber, avocado and coriander on a serving platter. Serve with the yogurt mixture and pistachios.

85 Interesting Salad

Ingredients

- ½ red cabbage, shredded
- 1 carrot, peeled, thinly sliced
- 3 green onions, thinly sliced diagonally
- 2 mangoes, sliced
- ½ tablespoon olive oil
- ½ avocado, peeled, thinly sliced
- ¼ cup fresh lime juice
- ¼ cup fresh orange juice
- salt and black pepper, to taste

Cooking

- Place oil, lime juice and orange juice in a small bowl. Season with salt and pepper. Whisk 2 minutes.
- Place the cabbage, carrot, onion, avocado and mango in a large bowl. Gently toss to combine. Drizzle with the dressing and serve.

86 Carrot & Cucumber Salad

Ingredients

- 2 carrots, peeled, cut into matchsticks
- 2 green shallots, thinly sliced diagonally
- 2 Lebanese cucumbers, quartered
- 1 tablespoon soy sauce
- 1 tablespoon fresh lemon juice
- salt and black pepper, to taste

Cooking

- Place the soy sauce, lemon juice, pepper and salt to the bowl. Whisk to combine. Set aside for 5 minutes.
- Then add the carrot, shallot, cucumber to the bowl, toss to combine. Serve.

87 Asparagus & Onion Salad

Ingredients

- 150g sour cream
- 1 tablespoon wholegrain mustard
- 2 tablespoons extra virgin olive oil
- 3 tablespoons fresh flat-leaf parsley, finely chopped
- 3 tablespoons fresh dill, finely chopped
- 1 bunch asparagus, woody stalks trimmed
- 5 spring onions, trimmed
- salt and black pepper, to taste

Cooking

- Whisk sour cream, mustard, 1 tablespoon oil, salt and pepper in a small bowl. Set aside.
- Prepare a barbecue or a grill for high heat. On a baking tray, toss asparagus and spring onions with 1 tablespoon olive oil and season with salt and pepper. Barbecue vegetables, turning as needed, for 5 minutes or until asparagus is lightly charred and crisp-tender.
- Spread mustard cream on bottom of a large serving platter. Place barbecued vegetables on top and add dill and parsley. Serve.

88 Rocket & Strawberry Salad

Ingredients

- 200g Coles Brand Australian Baby Rocket
- 100g strawberries, thinly sliced
- 5 red radishes, thinly sliced
- 1 teaspoon honey
- 1 tablespoons red wine vinegar
- 1 tablespoons extra virgin olive oil
- salt and black pepper, to taste

Cooking

- To make the dressing, place strawberry, oil, vinegar and honey in a bowl. Use a fork to crush. Combine and season.
- Arrange rocket and radish on the serving plates. Drizzle with dressing. Toss to combine. Serve.

89 Pumpkin & Apple Salad

Ingredients

- 400g butternut pumpkin, peeled, cut into 1cm thick chunks
- olive oil spray
- 50g baby spinach leaves
- 2 tablespoons extra virgin olive oil
- 3 apples, peeled, cut into 1cm thick chunks
- salt, cinnamon or vanilla, to taste

Cooking

- Preheat oven to 200C. Line a baking tray with baking paper. Arrange pumpkin in a single layer on tray. Spray oil on all sides. Roast for 30-35 minutes until tender. Remove and set aside to cool.
- Place the pumpkin, apple and spinach in a big bowl. Drizzle with oil. Season to taste. Gently toss to combine. Serve.

90 Apple & Red Cabbage Salad

Ingredients

- 1 small red cabbage
- ½ small red onion, finely grated
- 1 large carrot, peeled, grated
- ½ cup Coles light sour cream
- 1 tablespoon lemon juice
- 1 tablespoon olive oil
- 2 apples, peeled, cut into 1cm thick chunks
- salt and black pepper, to taste

Cooking

- Finely shred the cabbage. Place into a large bowl. Add onion, apple and carrot. Toss to combine.
- To make dressing, combine sour cream and lemon juice in a bowl. Season with salt and pepper. Whisk until combined. Drizzle dressing over cabbage mixture, toss to combine and serve.

91 Fantastic Green Salad

Ingredients

- 1 medium broccoli
- 2 large green apples, thinly sliced
- 1 mango, peeled, thinly sliced
- 1 tablespoon cider vinegar
- 1 tablespoon extra virgin olive oil
- 1 tablespoon finely chopped fresh mint
- ½ cup chopped walnuts
- salt and black pepper, to taste

Cooking

- Remove florets from broccoli stalk.
- Place broccoli florets, apple and mango in a bowl. Toss to combine.
- Place vinegar, oil and mint in a small bowl. Season with salt and pepper. Whisk to combine.
- Arrange broccoli, apple and mango on a platter. Drizzle with dressing. Sprinkle with walnuts. Serve.

92 Tuna Salad

Ingredients

- 125g can tuna in springwater, drained
- 6 cherry tomatoes, halved
- 60g baby spinach
- 1 Lebanese cucumbers, cut into 1cm thick chunks
- 1 tablespoon lemon juice
- 1 tablespoon apple juice
- salt and black pepper, to taste

Cooking

- Place tuna, tomato, cucumber and spinach in a bowl. Toss to combine.
- Combine lemon juice and apple juice in a small bowl. Season. Whisk to combine.
- Drizzle over the salad. Serve.

93 Spinach Salad

Ingredients

- 100g baby spinach
- ½ small red onion, finely grated
- 2 celery sticks, sliced
- 1 apple, thinly sliced
- 2 tablespoons light sour cream
- 1 teaspoon white wine vinegar
- 1 teaspoon honey
- 2 tablespoons chives, finely chopped
- salt and black pepper, to taste

Cooking

- Combine spinach, onion, celery and apple on a serving platter. Season with salt and pepper.
- Whisk sour cream, vinegar, honey and chives in a small jug. Season. Drizzle salad with dressing. Serve.

94 Seafood Salad

Ingredients

- 300g baby squid hoods, cleaned, scored, cut into 2cm pieces
- 1 tablespoon extra virgin olive oil
- 2 tablespoons mayonnaise
- 1 red onion, thinly sliced
- 150g cherry tomatoes, halved
- 5 radishes, thinly sliced
- 300g cooked prawns, peeled, tails intact
- ¼ cup lime juice
- salt and black pepper, to taste

Cooking

- Combine the squid and oil in a bowl. Season.
- Combine the onion, tomato, radishes, prawns, lime juice and mayonnaise in a bowl. Toss to combine.
- Add the squid, transfer to a plate and serve.

95 Asparagus, Radish & Apple Salad

Ingredients

- 1 bunch asparagus, trimmed
- 150g snow peas, trimmed
- ¼ cup fresh coriander leaves, chopped
- 2 green onions, thinly sliced
- 1 tablespoon lemon juice
- 1 tablespoon extra virgin olive oil
- 1 apple, thinly sliced
- 4 radishes, thinly sliced
- salt and black pepper, to taste

Cooking

- Bring a saucepan of water to the boil over high heat. Add asparagus. Cook for 2 minutes or until bright green and tender. Drain. Refresh under cold water. Drain. Chop into pieces.
- Place snow peas, coriander, onion, lemon juice, oil, apple and radish in a large bowl. Season with salt and pepper. Add the asparagus. Toss to combine. Transfer to a serving plate. Serve.

96 Cucumber & Tomato Salad

Ingredients

- 2 ripe tomatoes, sliced
- 1 small red onion, finely sliced
- 2 Lebanese cucumbers, cut into 1cm thick chunks
- 1 tablespoon Coles brand Italian red wine vinegar
- 2 tablespoon extra virgin olive oil
- salt and black pepper, to taste

Cooking

- Arrange tomato slices and cucumber on a serving platter and top with onion.
- Drizzle vinegar and oil over salad, and season with salt and black pepper. Serve.

97 Baby Spinach & Carrot Salad

Ingredients

- 150g baby spinach, washed and dried
- 75g Greek feta, crumbled
- 1 carrot, grated
- 1 tablespoon lemon juice
- ¼ cup olive oil
- 1 clove garlic, crushed
- salt and black pepper, to taste

Cooking

- Combine baby spinach, carrot and feta in a large bowl.
- For the dressing, place lemon juice, oil and garlic in a small bowl and whisk to combine.
- Drizzle the dressing over the salad, and season with salt and pepper. Serve.

98 Prawns & Cucumber Salad

Ingredients

- 2 Lebanese cucumbers, cut into 1cm thick chunks
- 2 tablespoons dill, chopped
- 1 red onion, finely sliced
- 1 garlic clove, crushed
- 2 tablespoon fresh lemon juice
- 300g Australian raw king prawns, peeled, tails intact
- 2 tablespoon olive oil
- salt and black pepper, to taste

Cooking

- Heat barbecue grill plate, or a chargrill, to medium-high heat. Drizzle prawns with olive oil, and cook for about 4 minutes each side, or until cooked through.
- Combine cucumber, onion, dill, garlic, lemon juice and oil in a large bowl. Season.
- Arrange the cucumber salad and prawns on serving plates. Serve.

99 Radish & Greek Feta Salad

Ingredients

- 5 radishes, thinly sliced
- 1 tablespoon olive oil
- 1 teaspoon sweet paprika
- 50g pistachios, toasted, coarsely chopped
- 100g Greek feta, coarsely crumbled
- 3 tablespoons mint leaves, chopped
- 3 tablespoons parsley leaves, chopped
- salt and black pepper, to taste

Cooking

- Combine the paprika, mint, parsley and oil in a large bowl. Season.
- Place the radish and feta in a large bowl. Drizzle with dressing gently toss to combine. Add the pistachios. Serve.

100 Tomato & Apple Salad

Ingredients

- 200g Perino grape tomatoes, halved
- 2 tablespoons extra-virgin olive oil
- 1 tablespoon fresh lemon juice
- 100g baby rocket leaves
- 1 tablespoon fresh basil leaves, torn
- 1 tablespoon fresh oregano leaves
- 1 apple, cut into 1,5cm thick chunks
- salt and black pepper, to taste

Cooking

- In a medium bowl, place the grape tomatoes, oil and lemon juice. Season with salt and pepper.
- In a bowl, toss the apple, rocket, basil and oregano. Season with salt and pepper. Scatter the rocket mixture over tomatoes and serve.

Milton Keynes UK
Ingram Content Group UK Ltd.
UKHW020614260224
438485UK00009B/165